W9-AES-481

JOE MAUER

BY BRIAN HOWELL

Published by ABDO Publishing Company, 8000 West 78th Street, Edina, Minnesota 55439. Copyright © 2011 by Abdo Consulting Group, Inc. International copyrights reserved in all countries. No part of this book may be reproduced in any form without written permission from the publisher. SportsZone™ is a trademark and logo of ABDO Publishing Company.

Printed in the United States of America,
North Mankato, Minnesota
112010
012011

 THIS BOOK CONTAINS AT LEAST 10% RECYCLED MATERIALS.

Editor: Matt Tustison
Copy Editor: Susan M. Freese
Interior Design and Production: Craig Hinton
Cover Design: Craig Hinton

Photo Credits: Jim Prisching/AP Images, cover, 1; Morry Gash/AP Images, 4; Tom Olmscheid/AP Images, 7, 23; Steven Senne/AP Images, 8; Paul Battaglia/AP Images, 10, 24; Star Tribune, Jennifer Simonson/AP Images, 13; Tom Dahlin /Sports Illustrated/Getty Images, 14; Tom Dahlin/Getty Images, 17; Ezra Shaw/Getty Images, 18; Jim Mone/AP Images, 20; Nati Harnik/AP Images, 26, 29

Library of Congress Cataloging-in-Publication Data

Howell, Brian, 1974-
  Joe Mauer : all-star catcher / by Brian Howell.
    p. cm. — (Playmakers)
  ISBN 978-1-61714-749-4
  1. Mauer, Joe, 1983—Juvenile literature. 2. Baseball players—United States—Biography—Juvenile literature. 3. Minnesota Twins (Baseball team)—Biography—Juvenile literature. I. Title.
  GV865..M376H68 2011
  796.357092—dc22
  [B]
                                    2010045858

TABLE OF CONTENTS

Joe Mauer

CHAPTER 1

HOMETOWN HERO

Joe Mauer always dreamed of becoming a professional athlete. He was born in St. Paul, Minnesota. He grew up as a big fan of the Minnesota Twins baseball team.

The Twins play in Minneapolis, which is just across the Mississippi River from St. Paul. St. Paul and Minneapolis are called the Twin Cities.

When Joe was a kid, stars such as Kirby Puckett and Kent Hrbek were popular players for the Twins.

Joe Mauer swings in 2010. Mauer is living his dream of being a pro athlete with his hometown Minnesota Twins.

Joe isn't the only member of his family who has played for the Twins organization. His two older brothers, Jake and Bill, were minor league players for the Twins. Jake was an infielder, and Bill was a pitcher. Neither one made it to the big leagues. But Jake became a minor league manager for the Twins.

Joe watched Hrbek and Puckett help the Twins win the World Series twice. The Twins won in 1987 when Joe was just four years old. They won again in 1991 when Joe was eight years old.

Joe worked hard to become a great athlete. He was a standout in several sports. But baseball was his favorite. Today, he is a member of the Twins. He lives out his dream of being a pro athlete every day. That he gets to do so for his hometown team makes it extra special.

Kids in Minnesota now dream of growing up to be like Mauer. He has become one of the best players in all of Major League Baseball (MLB). The Twins drafted Mauer straight out of high school in 2001. He made it through the minor leagues and to the major leagues by the start of the 2004 season.

Many baseball followers said Mauer was one of the most talented players they had seen in years. In 2009, Mauer had his

Mauer hits during the 2009 season. That year, he won the AL MVP Award and a third batting championship.

best year in the majors. He was so good that he was named the Most Valuable Player (MVP) of the American League (AL). Mauer finished the season with a .365 batting average, 28 home runs, and 96 runs batted in (RBIs).

"A dream of mine was always to play in the big leagues, and I got there," Mauer said. "Now to think I'm an MVP, I can't really describe it."

Mauer and Twins general manager Bill Smith smile in March 2010. Mauer was signing an eight-year, $184 million contract.

Mauer also won the AL batting title in 2009. This meant that he had the best batting average of all the players in the league. Mauer won three batting titles in the first five full seasons of his career. He also won batting crowns in 2006 and 2008.

But Mauer isn't only an outstanding hitter. He is also a talented defensive player. He plays catcher. This is an important

Through 2010, Mauer was one of only three catchers in baseball to ever win a batting title, and he was the only catcher to do it three times. He was also the only AL catcher to ever win a batting crown. Two National League (NL) catchers had won batting titles. Eugene Hargrave won in 1926, and Ernie Lombardi won in 1938 and 1942.

and difficult position. Catchers have to work closely with pitchers to help them succeed. In addition, catchers need to have a strong throwing arm to prevent runners from stealing bases. In November 2010, Mauer won his third AL Gold Glove Award in a row for his excellent defense.

So far, Mauer has had a great career with the Twins. Through the 2010 season, he had not yet won a World Series. But the Twins had been to the playoffs three times with Mauer.

Mauer loves playing for the Twins. Before the 2010 season, he signed an eight-year, $184 million contract that will keep him playing for his hometown team through the 2018 season. It was the richest contract ever given to a catcher.

"I have to tell everybody here I'll give you everything I've got," Mauer said at a news conference. "My ultimate goal is to win a World Series. I'm looking forward to doing that."

Joe Mauer

CHAPTER 2

CHILDHOOD

Joe Mauer was born on April 19, 1983, in St. Paul, Minnesota. His parents, Jake Jr. and Teresa, had three boys. Jake III was the oldest, followed by Bill. Joe was the youngest.

As a kid, Joe loved being around his older brothers. "Joe tagged along with Jake and Bill an awful lot," Joe's dad said. When the boys played together, they often played sports. All three loved baseball and played it very well.

Mauer and his dad, Jake Jr., are shown in 2010 after Jake Jr. threw the first pitch before a Twins home game.

When Joe was a child, his grandfather lived with the family. Jake Sr. helped Joe, Jake, and Bill grow up. He also taught the boys a lot about baseball. Jake Sr. was a minor league baseball player in his younger days. He taught Joe that if he could hit, he would always have a place to play on the baseball field.

Joe's father invented a tool that helped Joe practice his hitting in the family garage. The tool was a V-shaped pipe with holes on both ends. Joe would drop a baseball into one end of the pipe, and it would roll out of the other end. When the ball came out, Joe would swing his bat and hit the ball into a tarp. Joe often practiced by using a golf ball instead of a baseball. And instead of a bat, he used a steel pipe.

Using the tool helped Joe practice his swing. He learned how to swing quickly. Joe still credits that tool with helping him become the hitter he is today.

When Joe became a professional, his dad's invention received attention. Today, Mauer's Quickswing is a hot item for young baseball players. A lot of them use it to become better hitters.

Mauer, *bottom middle*, poses with some of his family members in November 2009 after he was named AL MVP.

From a young age, Joe was a great baseball player. When he was four years old, he already played much better than other kids his age. He got kicked out of his T-ball league because he hit the ball too hard.

Baseball wasn't the only sport Joe loved. He was also a great basketball player and a great football player. He kept playing all three of these sports into his teenage years.

Joe Mauer

CHAPTER 3

A HIGH SCHOOL STAR

Joe Mauer was a great athlete as a kid. But he became a legendary athlete in high school. Joe went to Cretin-Derham Hall (CDH) High School in St. Paul.

Many great athletes have attended CDH. Baseball Hall of Famer Paul Molitor went there. He played in the majors from 1978 to 1998 and was a standout for three teams. One of those teams was the Minnesota Twins. Chris Weinke also graduated

Joe prepares to pass the football in November 2000 during his senior season at Cretin-Derham Hall High School.

> Joe struck out only once during his entire high school career. That strikeout came during his junior year in the state tournament. The Raiders were playing a consolation game against Elk River High School. "Our bench got real quiet," said Jim O'Neill, Joe's coach at CDH. "Nobody said a thing. *Did you see what I just saw?*"

from CDH. He won the 2000 Heisman Trophy at Florida State University as college football's best player. Weinke also played minor league baseball before he enrolled at Florida State.

Joe might have been the best CDH athlete of them all, however. Just like his grandpa, Joe was a star in three sports during high school.

Playing for the CDH Raiders, Joe was a standout in basketball. He made the school's varsity team as a sophomore. During his junior and senior seasons, he was the team's leading scorer. He was also selected to the All-State basketball team both seasons. Joe helped CDH reach Minnesota's state tournament in his final year of high school. The Raiders finished in third place.

Joe was an outstanding football player too. He played quarterback for CDH. He made the varsity team as a junior.

Mauer, who was a football star in high school, waves to the crowd at a Minnesota Vikings game in 2007.

That year, he threw for 32 touchdowns and led the Raiders to a 13–0 record and their first state championship. During his senior year, Joe threw for 3,022 yards and 41 touchdowns. Joe led CDH back to the state title game. But the Raiders lost. Still, he was so good that the *USA Today* newspaper named him the national football player of the year.

Joe was a great basketball and football player. But he was even better at baseball. Baseball was always Joe's first love.

Jake Mauer, Joe's oldest brother, is shown in March 2004 when he was a minor leaguer in the Twins organization.

Joe made the CDH varsity baseball team as a sophomore. Joe excelled in his high school career. During his senior year, he had an amazing .605 batting average. With Joe leading the way, the Raiders won the state baseball championship in 2001.

After Joe's senior season, *USA Today* named him the national baseball player of the year. He was the first athlete to be named player of the year by *USA Today* in two sports.

Joe was featured in *Sports Illustrated* magazine while he was in high school. He was one of the magazine's "Faces in the Crowd" because of his accomplishments.

During high school, Joe also played for the US junior national baseball team for three years. He was named the best hitter at the world tournament in 2000.

It shouldn't have surprised anyone that Joe became a great athlete. His brothers were great athletes too. So were his grandfather and his grandfather's brothers. Joe's mom, Teresa, played basketball and volleyball in high school. Teresa's sister, Jean Tierney, played the same sports and made it into the sports Hall of Fame at Creighton University in Nebraska. One of Joe's cousins, Mark Mauer, played quarterback at the University of Nebraska in the 1980s. Another cousin, Ken Mauer, has been a longtime referee in the National Basketball Association (NBA).

Because Joe was such a talented athlete at CDH, he had several options for what to do after high school. But deciding which sport he would play in the future would be tough.

CHAPTER 4

BECOMING A TWIN

Joe Mauer had a difficult decision to make as he finished high school.

He was a star in football. Several colleges wanted him to play quarterback for their teams. He had decided that if he played football, he would play for Florida State University. Former CDH standout Chris Weinke had starred at Florida State. Professional baseball teams also wanted Mauer. Many scouts had watched his games at CDH.

Mauer puts on a Twins jersey on June 5, 2001. That day, the team chose Mauer first in baseball's amateur draft.

MLB held its draft soon after Mauer finished high school. The first pick in the draft went to Mauer's favorite team, the Minnesota Twins. The Twins selected the hometown kid. By that point, Mauer had made it clear that he wanted to play baseball.

Mauer played in the Twins' minor league system for the next three years. As always, he played very well. Then the Twins moved him up to their big-league team.

Opening Day of the 2004 season was April 5. In his first big-league game, Mauer went 2-for-3 during the Twins' 7–4 home victory over the Cleveland Indians in 11 innings.

Unfortunately, Mauer injured his left knee in just his second major league game. He had to sit out much of the rest of the 2004 season. But he still hit .308 with six home runs in 35 games.

Mauer was healthier in 2005. He batted .294 with nine homers and 55 RBIs in 131 games. In 2006, Mauer really proved himself to be a top player. He made the AL All-Star team for the first time. And at the end of the season, he was in a tough battle with New York Yankees star Derek Jeter for the league's batting title. The winner wasn't decided until the last day of the season. Mauer had two hits and finished with a .347 batting average.

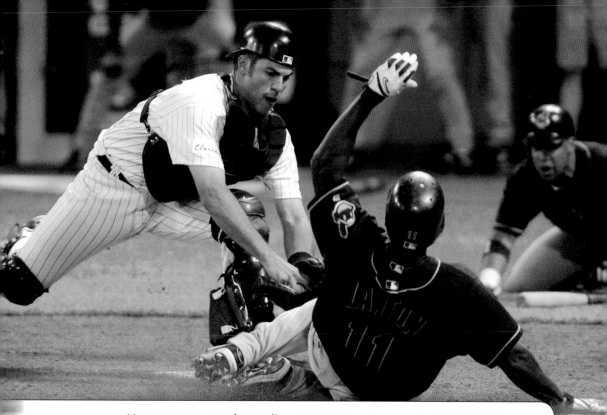

Mauer tags out the Indians' Matt Lawton on April 5, 2004. Mauer had two hits and two walks in his big-league debut.

Jeter had just one hit and finished with a .343 average. After the game, Mauer admitted that he had really wanted to win the batting crown. "I've never been so nervous in my life," he said.

Mauer was becoming one of MLB's brightest stars. He batted .293 in 2007. Then he hit .328 in 2008 and .365 in 2009. He won batting titles in both seasons. His .365 average was the highest ever for a catcher.

Mauer holds his 2009 AL MVP Award as he appears with ex-Twins stars Tony Oliva, *left*, and Harmon Killebrew in 2010.

Playing catcher is physically difficult. Crouching behind the plate so much is hard on catchers' knees. Foul balls also sometimes hit them. But Mauer proved he could be a strong, reliable catcher while also being an amazing hitter.

Mauer missed the first month of the 2009 season because of an injury to his back. But when he returned, he hit a home run in his first at-bat. Mauer went on to have his best season yet. It ended with him winning the AL MVP Award. Star first baseman Justin Morneau was happy to hear that Mauer, his good friend, had won the 2009 MVP honor. "He deserves it," Morneau said.

Mauer was well rewarded for his MVP season. The Twins gave him a new contract to make sure he would stay with the team for a long time. In 2010, Mauer hit .327 and helped Minnesota win the AL Central title for the second straight year and the third time in his six full big-league seasons.

The Twins had enjoyed a lot of regular-season success with Mauer on the team. But for some reason, Minnesota struggled in the playoffs. As of 2010, the Twins had lost all three of their playoff series with Mauer on the team. In 2010, the New York Yankees swept the Twins in the AL Division Series (ALDS) for the second year in a row. "It's frustrating," Mauer said.

The Twins were still hopeful about the future. During the 2010 season, fans flocked to Target Field, the team's new ballpark in downtown Minneapolis. Hundreds of them were wearing jerseys with the name "Mauer" on the back. The Twins were happy to build their future around this hometown hero.

Joe Mauer

CHAPTER 5

OFF THE FIELD

Joe Mauer has enjoyed many great moments on the baseball field. Fans of the Minnesota Twins love watching him play. But Mauer is more than just a great player. He has made many fans happy off the field too. When Mauer isn't playing baseball, he enjoys helping other people.

One of Joe's good friends growing up was Tony Leseman. Tony had a little brother, Mike, who had special needs. Some people treated Mike differently

Mauer plays in a charity golf tournament in Florida in 2010. Mauer believes in giving his time to help others.

Mauer likes to go to his log cabin in Minnesota when he isn't playing baseball. His cabin has a batting cage, so he can practice his hitting while he's there. The cabin also has a bowling alley. Mauer enjoys watching the deer while he's at his cabin.

because of his disabilities. But Joe became a good friend to Mike. Today, Joe, Tony, and Mike are still friends. Joe even helped Mike play a role in Tony's wedding in 2009.

People with disabilities sometimes have a hard time making friends. The Highland Friendship Club in Minnesota helps them make friends. Pat Leseman, the mother of Tony and Mike, started this club. Mauer volunteers his time to help. He even attends a bowling tournament every year to raise money for the club.

Mauer has helped people in other ways. He and his family have hosted a golf event every year since 2001. The event raises money for a group called Friends of St. Paul Baseball. The group helps kids who want to play baseball. The money raised by Mauer's golf event has also helped build baseball fields for kids.

Mauer signs autographs for fans at Twins spring training in Fort Myers, Florida, in February 2010.

During his career, Mauer has always been a hero to Twins fans on and off the field. Some star athletes don't like to sign autographs. But Mauer doesn't mind.

When Mauer was a kid, he always dreamed of playing for the Twins. Now he is living his dream. "I love putting on a Minnesota Twins uniform," he said. "It's a real thrill to be able to do this for the rest of my career."

FUN FACTS AND QUOTES

- Joe Mauer's parents, Jake Jr. and Teresa, had three boys. Each boy had different likes and dislikes. Joe hated washing dishes, so Teresa used that as a punishment for Joe when he got in trouble.

- One reason Mauer loves doing charity work is that he wants to give back to the people of St. Paul, where he grew up. "I think it's probably a little bit more special for me since this is my hometown," he said.

- Through the 2010 season, Mauer's career batting average of .327 was the third highest among all active MLB players. Only the St. Louis Cardinals' Albert Pujols and the Seattle Mariners' Ichiro Suzuki were ahead of Mauer. Both of those players had a lifetime average of .331.

- "When I'm up at the plate, it doesn't feel like anything is rushed. You see the ball coming in, and everything is nice and easy, and you put a good swing on it."
  —Mauer, on how he hits a baseball

WEB LINKS

To learn more about Joe Mauer, visit ABDO Publishing Company online at **www.abdopublishing.com**. Web sites about Mauer are featured on our Book Links page. These links are routinely monitored and updated to provide the most current information available.

GLOSSARY

batting average
A baseball statistic that tells how good a player is at hitting the ball. If a player gets four hits in 10 times at bat, he has a .400 batting average.

charity
Money given or work done to help people in need.

disabilities
Physical or mental limitations on what someone can do.

draft
In baseball, an event held every year in which teams take turns selecting new players.

league
In sports, a group of teams or clubs. Professional baseball teams are part of Major League Baseball (MLB). The MLB is divided into the American League (AL) and the National League (NL).

organization
In baseball, the different levels of teams that make up the whole franchise. The Twins organization has a major league team and several minor league teams.

professional
In sports, someone who is hired and gets paid to play his or her sport.

scouts
In sports, people who try to find talented players.

volunteer
To provide help or service without being paid.

INDEX

FURTHER RESOURCES

Berg, Steve, with Joe Mauer and Garrison Keillor. *Target Field: The New Home of the Minnesota Twins*. Minneapolis: MVP Books, 2010.

Brackin, Dennis, and Patrick Reusse, with Harmon Killebrew. *Minnesota Twins: The Complete Illustrated History*. Minneapolis: MVP Books, 2010.

Star Tribune. *Joe Mauer: From Hometown Hero to MVP*. Chicago: Triumph Books, 2010.

Wright, Dave. *162–0: The Greatest Wins in Twins History*. Chicago: Triumph Books, 2010.